Guidance
on Preparing A Complete & Sufficient Suspicious Activity Report Narrative

Financial Crimes Enforcement Network

Table of Contents

November 2003

Introduction

The purpose of the Suspicious Activity Report (SAR) is to report known or suspected violations of law or suspicious activity observed by financial institutions subject to the regulations of the Bank Secrecy Act (BSA). In many instances, SARs have been instrumental in enabling law enforcement to initiate or supplement major money laundering or terrorist financing investigations and other criminal cases. Information provided in SAR forms also presents the Department of the Treasury's Financial Crimes Enforcement Network (FinCEN) with a method of identifying emerging trends and patterns associated with financial crimes. The information about those trends and patterns is vital to law enforcement agencies and provides valuable feedback to financial institutions.[1]

Financial institutions are required to submit SAR forms that are complete, sufficient and timely filed. Unfortunately, some financial institutions file SAR forms that contain incomplete, incorrect, and/or disorganized narratives, making further analysis difficult, if not impossible. Some SAR forms are submitted with blank narratives. The failure to adequately describe the factors making the transaction or activity suspicious undermines the very purpose of the SAR and lessens its usefulness to law enforcement. Because the SAR narrative serves as the only free text area for summarizing suspicious activity, it is essential that financial institutions' staff write narratives that are clear, concise, and thorough.

Also, late filings, absence of supplementary SARs, and/or inaccuracies in SARs have an impact upon law enforcement's ability to determine whether a crime was committed or continues to be committed, and the extent of any possible criminal activity that has been committed. Therefore, it is imperative that financial institutions not only file complete and sufficient SARs but that those SARs are filed within the established deadlines.[2]

Many different financial industries are now required to file SARs. Each SAR form was specifically designed to accommodate respective institution types [e.g., depository institutions, money services businesses (MSBs), securities sector, etc.]. Despite the fact that these industries use different SAR formats, the basic structure for a SAR narrative remains the same. The purpose of *Guidance on Preparing A Complete & Sufficient Suspicious Activity Report Narrative* is to educate SAR filers on how to organize and write narrative details that maximizes the value of each SAR form by:

- using a simple methodology for evaluating and reporting information for the SAR narrative and why it is important;

---

[1] FinCEN provides feedback to financial institutions in the form of advisories, bulletins and other publications such as *The SAR Activity Review – Trends, Tips & Issues* and *By the Numbers*.

[2] A financial institution is required to file a SAR no later than 30 calendar days after the date of initial detection of facts that may constitute a basis for filing a SAR. If no suspect was identified on the date of detection of the incident requiring the filing, a financial institution may delay filing a SAR for an additional 30 calendar days to identify a suspect. In no case shall reporting be delayed more than 60 calendar days after the date of initial detection of a reportable transaction.

- providing a general guideline on how to organize the SAR narrative so that critical details are concise and follow a logical order of presentation; and

- providing respective industries with examples of sufficient and insufficient SAR narratives.

Information presented in this guidance document should be used in conjunction with the instructions provided with the appropriate SAR forms, guidance provided in other FinCEN publications (such as *The SAR Activity Review – Trends, Tips & Issues, FinCEN Advisory Issue 33: Informal Value Transfer Systems*), and respective industry advisories from the federal regulatory authorities. The information in *Guidance on Preparing A Complete & Sufficient Suspicious Activity Report Narrative* is provided solely to assist respective financial institutions in strengthening existing due diligence initiatives and anti-money laundering programs.

Collecting Information for the SAR Narrative

FinCEN provided some of this information in Issue 2 of The SAR Activity Review (June 2001). Additional information is being provided to address the unique challenges of the securities industry and state-of-the-art communication mechanisms that are commonly employed by criminals to facilitate the movement of funds.

The information generated from SAR filings plays an important role in identifying potential illegal activities such as money laundering and terrorist financing, and assists law enforcement in detecting and preventing the flow of illicit funds through our financial system. It is critical that the information provided in a SAR filing be as accurate and complete as possible. The SAR form should include any information readily available to the filing institution obtained through the account opening process and during due diligence efforts.

In general, a SAR narrative should identify the five essential elements of information – **who? what? when? where? and why?** – of the suspicious activity being reported. The method of operation (or how?) is also important and should be included in the narrative.

Who is conducting the suspicious activity?

While one section of the SAR form calls for specific suspect information,[3] the narrative should be used to further describe the suspect or suspects, including occupation, position or title within the business, and the nature of the suspect's business(es). If more than one individual or business is involved in the suspicious activity, identify all suspects and any known relationships amongst them in the Narrative Section. While detailed suspect information may not always be available (e.g., in situations involving non-account holders), such information should be included to the maximum extent possible. Addresses for suspects are important; filing institutions should note not only the suspect's primary street addresses, but also, other known addresses, including any post office box numbers and apartment numbers when applicable. Any identification numbers associated with the suspect(s) other than those provided earlier are also beneficial, such as passport, alien registration, and driver's license numbers.

What instruments or mechanisms are being used to facilitate the suspect transaction(s)?

An illustrative list of instruments or mechanisms that may be used in suspicious activity includes, but is not limited to, wire transfers, letters of credit and other trade instruments, correspondent accounts, casinos, structuring, shell companies, bonds/notes, stocks, mutual funds, insurance policies, travelers checks, bank drafts, money orders, credit/debit cards, stored value cards, and/or digital currency business services.

---

[3] Specific suspect identifying information is provided in Part II of the depository institution Suspicious Activity Report (SAR/TD F 90-22.47) and in Part I of the Suspicious Activity Report by Money Services Business (SAR-MSB/TD F 90-22.56), Suspicious Activity Report by the Securities and Futures Industries (SAR-SF Form/FinCEN Form 101), and the Suspicious Activity Report by Casinos and Card Clubs (SAR-C/FinCEN Form 102).

In addition, a number of different methods may be employed for initiating the negotiation of funds such as the Internet, phone access, mail, night deposit box, remote dial-up, couriers, or others. In summarizing the flow of funds, always include the source of the funds (origination) that lead to the application for, or recipient use of, the funds (as beneficiary). In documenting the movement of funds, identify all account numbers at the financial institution affected by the suspicious activity[4] and when possible, provide any account numbers held at other institutions and the names/locations of the other financial institutions, including MSBs and foreign institutions involved in the reported activity.

When did the suspicious activity take place?

If the activity takes place over a period of time, indicate the date when the suspicious activity was first noticed and describe the duration of the activity. Filers will often provide a tabular presentation of the suspicious account activities (transactions in and out). While this information is useful and should be retained, ***do not*** insert objects, tables, or pre-formatted spreadsheets when filing a SAR. These items may not convert properly when keyed in or merged into the SAR System. Also, in order to better track the flow of funds, individual dates and amounts of transactions should be included in the narrative rather than just the aggregated amount.

Where did the suspicious activity take place?

Use the Narrative Section to indicate that multiple offices of a single financial institution were involved in the suspicious activity and provide the addresses of those locations.

Specify if the suspected activity or transaction(s) involve a foreign jurisdiction. If so, provide the name of the foreign jurisdiction, financial institution, address and any account numbers involved in, or affiliated with the suspected activity or transaction(s).

Why does the filer think the activity is suspicious?

We suggest that you first describe briefly your industry or business – depository institution, casino, mortgage broker, securities broker, insurance, real estate, investment services, money remitter, check casher, etc. Then describe, as fully as possible, why the activity or transaction is unusual for the customer; consider the types of products and services offered by your industry, and the nature and normally expected activities of similar customers.

---

[4] When the number of accounts exceeds the number of account blocks on the respective SAR form, use the Narrative Section of the SAR to identify the additional accounts and any other information that cannot be placed in other sections of the SAR form.

Examples of some common patterns of suspicious activity are:

- a lack of evidence of legitimate business activity, or any business operations at all, undertaken by many of the parties to the transaction(s);

- unusual financial nexuses and transactions occurring among certain business types (e.g., food importer dealing with an auto parts exporter);

- transactions that are not commensurate with the stated business type and/or that are unusual and unexpected in comparison with the volumes of similar businesses operating in the same locale;

- unusually large numbers and/or volumes of wire transfers and/or repetitive wire transfer patterns;

- unusually complex series of transactions indicative of layering activity involving multiple accounts, banks, parties, jurisdictions;

- suspected shell entities;

- bulk cash and monetary instrument transactions;

- unusual mixed deposits of money orders, third party checks, payroll checks, etc., into a business account;

- transactions being conducted in bursts of activities within a short period of time, especially in previously dormant accounts;

- transactions and/or volumes of aggregate activity inconsistent with the expected purpose of the account and expected levels and types of account activity conveyed to the financial institution by the accountholder at the time of the account opening;

- beneficiaries maintaining accounts at foreign banks that have been subjects of previous SAR filings;

- parties and businesses that do not meet the standards of routinely initiated due diligence and anti-money laundering oversight programs (e.g., unregistered/unlicensed businesses);

- transactions seemingly designed to, or attempting to avoid reporting and recordkeeping requirements; and

- correspondent accounts being utilized as "pass-through" points by foreign jurisdictions with subsequent outgoing funds to another foreign jurisdiction.[5]

How did the suspicious activity occur?

Use the Narrative Section to describe the "modus operandi" or the method of operation of the subject conducting the suspicious activity. In a concise, accurate and logical manner, describe how the suspect transaction or pattern of transactions was committed. Provide as completely as possible a full picture of the suspicious activity involved. For example, if what appears to be structuring of currency deposits is matched with outgoing wire transfers from the accounts, the SAR narrative should include information about both the structuring and outbound transfers (including dates, destinations, amounts, accounts, frequency, and beneficiaries of the funds transfers).

---

[5] Other examples of suspicious activity may be found in previously published FinCEN Advisories, SAR Bulletins, and editions of *The SAR Activity Review – Trends, Tips & Issues,* all which may be found on the FinCEN website, www.fincen.gov. Also, some BSA Examination Manuals issued by the federal financial regulatory authorities include lists of potential suspicious activity. For example, refer to Section 1001.0 of the Federal Reserve Board's BSA Examination Manual (September 1997), www.federalreserve.gov/boarddocs/supmanual; page 12-18 of the OCC's BSA/Anti-Money Laundering Comptroller's Handbook (September 2000), www.occ.treas.gov/handbook/compliance htm; or Attachment 18.1 of Chapter 18 in the National Credit Union Administration's Examiner's Guide, www.ncua.gov/ref/examiners guide/. The other regulatory authorities [Federal Deposit Insurance Corporation (FDIC), Office of Thrift Supervision (OTS), Securities and Exchange Corporation (SEC), and the Internal Revenue Service (IRS)] may also provide guidance to you.

Organizing Information in the SAR Narrative

When all applicable information is gathered, analyzed, and documented and the financial institution decides that a SAR is required, the information should be described in the SAR Narrative in a concise and chronological format. Include all elements of the five W's *(Who? What? When? Where? and Why?)* previously discussed in Section 1 of this document, as well as any other information that can assist law enforcement.

We suggest that you divide the narrative into three sections: an introduction, a body, and a conclusion.

Introduction:

The introductory paragraph can provide:

- the purpose of the SAR and a general description of the known or alleged violation [In some instances, this might warrant mentioning at the outset the type of suspicious activity being observed, such as Informal Value Transfer System (IVTS) operations, smurfing, shell entities, complex layering activities, structuring, check kiting, embezzlement, etc.];

- the date of any SAR(s) filed previously on the suspect or related suspects and the reason why the previous SAR(s) was filed;

- whether the SAR is associated with the Office of Foreign Assets Control's (OFAC) sanctioned countries or Specially Designated Nationals and Blocked Persons or other government lists for individuals or organizations;

- any internal investigative numbers used by the financial institution which may be a point of reference for law enforcement should the investigators wish to contact the institution; and

- a summary of the "red flags" and suspicious patterns of activity that initiated the SAR. (This information should be provided either in the introduction or conclusion of the narrative.)

Body:

The next paragraph or paragraphs of the narrative can provide all pertinent information – supporting why the SAR was filed and might include:

- any and all relevant facts about the parties (individuals and businesses) who facilitated the suspicious activity or transactions. Include any unusual observations such as suspected shell entities; financial activities which are not commensurate with the expected normal business flows and types of transactions; unusual multiple party relationships; customer verbal statements; unusual and/or complex series of transactions indicative of layering; lack of business justification and documentation supporting the activity; etc.;

- a specific description of the involved accounts and transactions, identifying if known, both the origination and application of funds (usually identified in chronological order by date and amount);

- breaking out larger volumes of financial activity into categories of credits and debits, and by date and amount;

- transactor and beneficiary information, providing as much detail as possible, including the name and location of any involved domestic and/or international financial institution(s); names, addresses, account numbers, and any other available identifiers of originator and beneficiary transactor(s) and/or third parties or business entities on whose behalf the conductor was acting; the date(s) of the transaction(s); and amount(s);

- an explanation of any observed relationships among the transactors (e.g., shared accounts, addresses, employment, known or suspected business relationships and/or frequency of transactions occurring amongst them; appearing together at the institution and/or counter);

- specific details on cash transactions that identify the branch(es) where the transaction(s) occurred, the type of transaction(s), and how the transaction(s) occurred (e.g., night deposit, on-line banking, ATM, etc.); and

- any factual observations or incriminating statements made by the suspect.

Conclusion:

The final paragraph of the narrative can summarize the report and might also include:

- information about any follow-up actions conducted by the financial institution (e.g., intent to close or closure of accounts, ongoing monitoring of activity, etc.);

- names and telephone numbers of other contacts at the financial institution if different from the point of contact indicated in the SAR;

- a general description of any additional information related to the reported activity that may be made available to law enforcement by the institution; and

- names of any law enforcement personnel investigating the complaint who are not already identified in another section of the SAR.

Important Reminder:

Please do not include any supporting documentation with your filed report nor use the terms "see attached" in the Narrative Section. When SAR forms are received at the IRS Detroit Computing Center (DCC), only information that is in an explicit, narrative format is keypunched; thus, tables, spreadsheets or other attachments are not entered into the SAR System database. Keep any supporting documentation in your institution's records for five years. Law enforcement will contact you at the appropriate time to review any additional information.

Appendices

Examples of Sufficient and Insufficient SAR Narratives

In an effort to provide helpful guidance to financial institutions, FinCEN reviewed the SAR System database to identify previously submitted SARs that contained sufficient and complete narratives as well as insufficient or incomplete narratives. We are providing examples of sanitized sufficient and insufficient SARs submitted from different types of industries currently required to file SARs (depository institutions, MSBs, brokers or dealers in securities, and casinos and card clubs) as well as a few hypothetical SARs for illustration. Each example is followed by a brief commentary on the narrative.

Examples of SARs Filed by Depository Institutions

Sufficient and Complete Depository Institution SAR Narratives

Example #1

Investigation case number: A5678910. The customer, a grocery store and its owner, are suspected of intentionally structuring cash deposits to circumvent federal reporting requirements. The customer is also engaged in activity indicative of an informal value transfer operation: deposits of bulk cash, third party out of state personal checks and money orders, and engaging in aggregate wire transfers to Dubai, UAE. The type and volume of activity observed is non-commensurate with the customer's expected business volume and deviates from the normal volume of similar types of businesses located in the same area as the customer. Investigative activities are continuing. Our bank has elected to directly contact law enforcement concerning this matter along with filing this SAR.

John Doe opened a personal checking account, #12345-6789, in March of 1994. Doe indicated that he was born in Yemen, presented a Virginia driver's license as identification, and claimed he was the self-employed owner of a grocery store identified as Acme, Inc. A business checking account, #23456-7891, was opened in January of 1998 for Acme, Inc.

Between January 17, 2003, and March 21, 2003, John Doe was the originator of nine wires totaling $225,000. The wire transfers were always conducted at the end of each week in the amount of $25,000. All of the wires were remitted to the Bank of Anan in Dubai, UAE, to benefit Kulkutta Building Supply Company, account #3489728.

Reviews covering the period between January 2 and March 17, 2003, revealed that 13 deposits (consisting of cash, checks, money orders) totaling approximately $50,000 posted to the personal account. Individual amounts ranged between $1,500 and $9,500 and occurred on consecutive business days in several instances. A number of third-party out of state checks and money orders were also deposited into the account.

A review of deposit activity on the Acme, Inc. account covering the same period revealed 33 deposits (consisting of cash, checks, money orders) totaling approximately $275,000. Individual amounts ranged between $4,446 and $9,729; however 22 of 33 deposits ranged between $9,150 and $9,980. It was further noted that in nine of 13 instances in which cash deposits were made to both accounts on the same day, the combined deposits of cash exceeded $10,000. The bank filed currency transaction reports to the IRS for all aggregate daily transactions exceeding $10,000.

A search of the world wide web identified a website for Acme, Inc., which identified the company as a grocery store that provides remittance services to countries in the Middle East that includes Iran (an OFAC blocked country). Contact with the Virginia State Department of Banking indicates Acme, Inc. is not a licensed money wire transfer business. The bank will close this account because of the suspect nature of the transactions being conducted by John Doe.

Comments:

This narrative is a well-written summary of all the suspicious activity and supports the stated purpose for filing the SAR. Furthermore, the narrative provides an internal bank reference number for the SAR that can be used by law enforcement should investigators wish to contact the bank to discuss pertinent facts presented in the narrative. Specific information is also provided in the narrative that details the source and application of suspect funds. The SAR also identifies other actions taken by the financial institution as part of its internal due diligence program and its efforts in detecting possible illegal activity being facilitated by the suspect.

Example #2

Doe's Auto Sales, commercial checking account #1234567, is being reported for unusual activity and structured cash deposits. Doe's Auto Sales operates as a small used car lot with an inventory of less than 10 vehicles at any given time. John Doe is the owner of Doe's Auto Sales and a signer on the account. Jane Doe is an additional signer. The account was opened in September 2002 at the Happy Valley branch in Anytown, CA.

Account activity is usually extremely limited and several months involve periods of no account activity. However, many suspicious and structured transactions were conducted in June 2003 at two different bank branches in Anytown. The cash deposits were conducted in a manner possibly to avoid filing a currency transaction report. The structured cash deposits were always conducted for $9,800 each. Immediately following each deposit, a check for $9,800 posted to the account, payable to Doe's Auto Sales. Those checks were deposited to an account at XYZ Bank, also located in Anytown. Structured cash deposits conducted in June 2003 were as follows: 06/03 $9,800; 06/04 $9,800; 06/09 $9,800; 06/10 $9,800; 06/11 $9,800; and 06/12 $9,800. The deposits on 06/03, 06/09, and 06/11 were completed at the Happy Valley branch by John Doe. The remaining deposits, on 06/04, 06/10, and 6/12, were conducted by Jane

Doe at the Main Office branch. The source of the cash deposited to the account is unknown.

Checks posting to the account payable to Doe's Auto Sales and deposited at XYZ bank were as follows: 06/04 $9,800; 06/05 $9,800; 06/10 $9,800; 06/11 $9,800, 06/12 $9.800; and 06/13 $9.800. It is unknown what happened to the funds after the deposits to XYZ Bank.

Due to the pattern and manner of recent transactions, it appears that the cash deposits to credit Doe's Auto Sales were structured to evade the reporting requirement of the Bank Secrecy Act. Additionally, the immediate movement of funds out of the bank to another financial institution in amounts slightly below $10,000 seems unusual. A review of prior transactions since the account opened revealed no similar type of activity or in such amounts. Therefore, this suspicious activity report is being submitted.

The bank will continue to monitor the account for further activity and file a supplemental SAR if required.

All documentation obtained during this investigation is located in the case file, case #03-501, maintained by the bank's anti-money laundering department. Additional branch location address: Main Office branch- 100 West Happy Valley Street, Anytown, CA 12345.

Comments:

Facts presented in this SAR narrative clearly support the purpose of the SAR filing and also provide a disposition on further actions by the financial institution. The location of documentation supporting the SAR is identified. The institution provides information related to previous banking activity and identifies the dates, amounts, and locations of specific transactions to establish the pattern of structured transactions.

Example #3

Bank investigation file number AA67325.

This SAR is being filed to summarize suspicious cash deposits and wire transfer activity conducted by John Doe, account #12345678910. John Doe has been a bank customer since April 2000. Mr. Doe is a college student and employed part-time at Quickie Car Wash.

Cash deposits to Mr. Doe's personal checking account are structured to possibly circumvent federal reporting requirements. The deposits are followed by immediate wire transfers to Aussie Bank in Sydney, Australia to a single beneficiary, Jennifer Doe, account #981012345, with an address located in Australia. Specifically the following activity has been observed: cash deposits (dates followed by amounts): 03/15/02

$9,950.00; 03/17/02 $9,700.00; 03/18/02 $10,000; total: $29,650. Wire transfers out (dates followed by amounts): 03/16/02 $9,900.00, 03/18/02 $9,700.00, 03/19/02 $9,900.00. The volume and frequency of the deposits is not consistent with previous banking transactions conducted by Mr. Doe. The amounts of currency do not appear consistent with the customer's stated employment. Also, the relationship between the customer and Jennifer Doe and the purpose for the wire activity is unknown.

Therefore, due to the structured cash deposits by the customer on almost consecutive days into the account, and the immediate wire transfer of the funds out of the account to Jennifer Doe, Aussie bank, account #891012345, Sydney Australia, this SAR is being filed. Investigation is continuing.

The bank's financial intelligence unit in Big City, FL, maintains all records related to this SAR.

Comments:

The narrative provides a sufficient explanation for the SAR filing in addition to providing an internal bank file number for law enforcement to reference if it wishes to contact the depository institution. Facts presented in the SAR narrative clearly support the purpose of the SAR filing. The narrative includes information on disposition on further actions by the financial institution and identifies the availability and location of documentation supporting the SAR.

Example #4

The Bank of Mainland (BM) filed an initial suspicious activity report (SAR) dated 6/11/01. The SAR was filed due to unusual wire transfer and cash deposit activity involving two BM corporate customers, Sky Corporation and Sea Corporation, both registered in Vermont and having a common Vermont address. BM has also filed numerous CTRs on cash deposits conducted on behalf of the two companies. Our previous and recent reviews of the customers' activities revealed the cash deposits and wire transfers involving the companies might be consistent with money laundering.

Because BM was unable to determine any particulars about the companies in order to establish a business justification for the activity, the following patterns appeared suspicious:

1. A repeating pattern of structured cash deposits into business accounts held by the companies with wire transfers to a particular beneficiary.
2. Individual transactions conducted in large dollar amounts.

3. Individual transactions conducted in even dollar amounts.
4. Individual transactions conducted within a short period of time (i.e., daily basis, 2x's daily, every other day).
5. Periodic incoming wire transfers from a foreign corporation via a correspondent account maintained by a foreign bank at Bank of Mainland.

Specifically, the analysis of the cash deposit and wire activity for the period 2/2/99 through 6/20/01 revealed the following:

1. The Vermont companies are as follows: Sky Corporation and Sea Corporation, both of 1234 North Harvard Street, Suite 81, in Burlington, Vermont.

2. The total number and dollar value of cash deposits into accounts held by the companies are as follows: Sky Corporation, account #54321098, 284 deposits totaling $2,710,000; Sea Corporation, account #12345678, 200 deposits totaling $1,900,000. Reviews of the accounts indicate all the deposits were night deposits conducted through three main branches of BM: North Burlington; South Burlington; and West Burlington. The average amount of deposits negotiated through account #12345678 was from $8,720 to $16,500. Many of the transactions conducted on the same day at multiple branches in amounts under $10,000 may have been conducted to circumvent federal reporting requirements.

3. 15 incoming wire transfers were received from Tolinka Inc. affecting account #12345678. Tolinka Inc. is registered in Utah and is a customer of Bank XYZ in Warsaw, Poland, account #689472. Bank XYZ maintains a correspondent relationship with the Bank of Poland. The Bank of Poland, in turn, maintains a correspondent account at BM. As part of BM's due diligence of foreign wire transactions, we contacted Bank of Poland to have them inquire with Bank XYZ about Tolinka Inc. Bank XYZ could not substantiate the type of business activity or provide any documentation for Tolinka Inc. Bank XYZ's contact with Tolinka Inc. in response to our query resulted in the business closing its account with Bank XYZ with no explanation provided.

4. The total number and dollar value of outgoing wire transfers from Sky Corporation and Sea Corporation is as follows: Sky Corporation, account #5431098, 274 wire transfer debits totaling $2,697,000; Sea Corporation, account #12345678, 198 wire transfer debits totaling $1,866,000. The day after cash deposits, wire transfers were usually conducted through the use of a remote computer terminal as part of an Internet service for the accounts. The amount of wire transfers usually equaled the aggregate of deposits from the day before. All

wire transfers from both accounts were remitted to Paul Lafonte, Artsy Bank, account #456781234, in Paris, France.

At the time the accounts were opened with our financial institution, a registered agent for both companies provided corporate filings filed with the Secretary of State of Vermont indicating the companies are for-profit, engaged in retail shoe sales. As part of our annual review of corporate accounts, we were unable to substantiate if the companies are still active from researching public records, commercial database systems, or the Internet. Attempted telephone contact with the companies identified both numbers as being disconnected. The companies do not appear to maintain operating businesses in Vermont; and there is no indication of legitimate business activity.

Due to these factors and the suspicious demeanor of the account activity, bank management has decided to end our banking relationships with Sky Corporation and Sea Corporation. All records related to this matter are being maintained by the bank's central branch operations officer in Burlington, VT.

Comments:

The narrative is a well-written summary identifying all aspects of the suspicious transactions conducted by the suspect businesses including the apparent structuring of cash deposits on multiple days at multiple branch locations, the use of a foreign account to facilitate wire transfers to the customer's accounts through a correspondent bank, and the use of online transactions to effect outgoing wire transfers. The depository institution documents its due diligence efforts to determine the status and operations of its suspicious customers as well as its efforts to glean information about the originator of the suspicious wire transfers. The financial institution indicates that CTRs (Currency Transaction Reports) and a SAR were filed previously. The institution conveys the disposition of the two accounts and the location where records are stored. (Note: Because of the volume of activity summarized in the narrative, a detailed listing of check numbers, senders, etc. is included in the originally filed SAR but omitted for the purpose of maintaining some brevity within the narrative for this report.)

Insufficient or Incomplete Depository Institutions SAR Narratives

Example #1

John Doe was the originator of nine wires totaling $225,000. All of the wires were remitted to a Dubai based company. During the same period of time John Doe deposited cash, money orders, and checks into his account. See attachment.

Comments:

This SAR fails to provide specific details on the application of the suspect funds (the name, bank, and account number of the beneficiary, if identifiable). The SAR also references an attachment, which is not available to the reader since supporting documents are not entered into the SAR System database. **(Please remember that attachments should not be sent with the SAR. Rather, any supporting documentation should be described in the SAR narrative and retained with the financial institution's case file.)** The depository institution fails to provide any information concerning the relationship, if any, between the institution and the customer. Also, no specific transaction data is provided that identifies the dates and amounts of each wire transfer.

Example #2

A.) Copy of the questionable activity report (QAR) from Bank Secrecy Act Department outlining the suspected structuring of cash-in activity by our customer, Management Services, a management company for the period of 07/10/02 to 07/22/02.   B.) Management Services, financially, via the suspected structuring of cash-in activity to avoid CTR reporting.   C.) N.A.   D.) See A. above.   E.) N.A.   F.) Downtown branch, 25 E. Third Street, Anytown, SD 12345.   G.) The activity consisted of 4 transactions for the month of July 2002.   H.) N.A.   I.) N.A.   J.) To the best of my knowledge, no information has been excluded from this report.   K.) Currency was involved.   L.) 224-307711.

Comments:

Although the bank responds to the checklist found in the SAR instructions, it fails to provide a chronological and complete account of the violation of law in order to explain the nature of the suspicious activity. The SAR fails to identify specific examples of the structuring activity, including dates and amounts of the transactions. Additionally, the filing bank does not explain if the deposits were consistent with the expected transactions of the business. Finally, the narrative does not identify what happened to the funds after they were deposited into the bank account.

Example #3

We believe this customer is structuring to avoid CTR filing.

Comments:

The bank does not provide any beneficial information in the narrative. It fails to relate the types of transactions (cash-in or cash-out), the amounts and dates, background information on the customer, source or dispersal of funds in customer's account, or other information to support the statement provided in the narrative.

Examples of SARs Filed by Money Services Businesses (SAR-MSBs)

Sufficient and complete SAR-MSB Narratives

Example #1

This SAR is being filed on three suspects who purchased money orders in a manner to circumvent federal identification and recording requirements and engaged in suspicious money order transactions.

On May 1, 2003, two male customers came into the North City store location of XYS Money Orders Express and attempted to purchase a total of $7,000 in money orders. Prior to seeing a clerk, both customers stood in line and were observed conversing as if they worked with each other. Both customers went to different clerks and each attempted to purchase $3,500 in money orders with cash. When each customer was asked for identification per the $3,000-$10,000 recording requirement, the customers abruptly decided to lower their money order purchases below $3,000. One of the customers requested to purchase $2,500 in money orders while the other requested to purchase $2,900 in money orders. Customer One, at window 1, was issued money orders, serial numbers /amounts: 112345/$1,500 and 112346/$1,000. The second customer, at window 2, was issued money orders 122347/$1,500 and 122348 for $1,400. The two individuals left together in a white Ford van.

Later that same day, the same suspects returned to the same store with a female companion. The female purchased $2,000 from window 2, serial numbers/amounts: 112412/$1,000 and 112413/$1,000. The three suspects left the building together and drove away in a red Porsche.

On May 2, 2003, the female suspect entered the South City store location and again purchased money orders totaling $2,500. The instruments were purchased from window 1, serial numbers/amounts: 113345/$1,500 and 113346/$1,000. The customer was observed being picked up by the two previously referenced male suspects in a red Porsche.

On May 2, 2003, the North City store contacted the South City store to advise them that two money orders, #112345 and 113345, purchased the day before at the South City and North City stores were being used to purchase six $500 international money orders totaling $3,000, #1125451, #1125452, #1125453, #1125454, #1125455, and #1125456 by two male customers.

Comments:

This narrative provides a complete summary of suspect money order purchases between two branches of a single money order seller. It provides the number of suspects involved, the interaction between those suspects, and the manner in which the money orders were purchased, including the serial numbers and respective denominations of the money orders. In addition, the narrative identifies communication between two MSB business locations on the possible layering of money orders used to purchase international money orders, perhaps to further complicate any possible audit trail of the original transaction.

Example #2

> For at least a year, beginning on May 20, 2002, two customers, John Doe and his son, Bob, have been using our money transmitter service to send large amounts of money (in cash) to receivers named Jane Smith and Mary Smith located in Antigua. Funds are sent to the XYZ Caribbean Money Center in St. Johns, Antigua. The amount of money presented each time by John and/or Bob Doe is usually $5000 and the transmittals are sent bi-weekly. During one particular incident earlier this month, on June 12, 2003, John Doe attempted to send $10,000 without proper identification. We refused to send the funds and Mr. Doe left the premises. He returned later in the afternoon with identification but only sent $5000. All incidents / transactions have occurred at our store in Anytown, IL. The office has documentation of the driver's licenses of both customers. Suspicion lies in the Does' occupation (lawyers), and the amount of money leading me to suspect possible tax evasion. Records related to the money transmittals are maintained in our store in Anytown.

Comments:

This narrative provides enough details of the MSB customers' frequent suspicious money transmittals to support the purpose of the SAR. Also, the beneficiary information, including beneficiary names and location, was included. The narrative identified the suspects by name and occupation and related that records, including driver's license information, were retained at the MSB business location.

Insufficient or incomplete SAR-MSB Narratives

Example #1

> Money orders were purchased on 12-19-02 to Smith Corporation in the amount of $6,500.00.

Comments:

No explanation is given as to why the MSB considers this activity suspicious. The filer does not indicate if money orders were purchased with cash. The filer fails to provide any information about the purchaser or nature of the business and if this activity was normal or unusual for the purchaser or business.

Example #2

> Any further transactions sent by this sender will be kept on file. We will not be sending a report for every transaction. Thank you.

Comments:

The narrative only provides a reference to an unknown subject -"this sender,"-- and fails to identify a possible violation. It gives no information on the amounts of the money transmittals or the beneficiary of the funds. The only value the narrative provides is to alert the reader that the MSB may be violating BSA regulations by not filing future SARs on additional suspicious activity that might be conducted by the subject.

Examples of SARs Filed by Broker-Dealers (SAR-SFs)

Sufficient and Complete SAR-SF Narratives

Example #1

On November 15, 2002, ABC Brokerage Firm, Office of General Counsel, filed a suspicious activity report for Jane Doe, account number 88112233. In summary, the prior submission reported that during the period of September 9, 2002 through October 1, 2002, Ms. Doe sent six wire transfers for amounts just under $10,000 each to her business account in Mexico.

After ABC Brokerage Firm management advised the client that they would no longer accept such wire transfer instructions, the client began cashing checks drawn on her ABC Brokerage Firm account at casas de cambio in Mexico. Specifically, on December 17 and 18, 2002, the client cashed three checks made payable to a casa de cambio for an aggregate total of $19,500. When asked the reason for preparing and cashing these checks in this manner, Ms. Doe claimed, in substance, that she did not want to fill out the paperwork required by Mexican law for cash transactions of U.S. $10,000 or more.

The account has been closed. Primary federal regulator – SEC

Comments:

The narrative provides information concerning a previously filed SAR. It also describes the suspect activity and actions taken by the broker-dealer.

Example # 2

Between November 1999 and September 2001, John Doe opened three accounts at our brokerage firm's branch office in Any City, NY. Mr. Doe was either the joint account holder or had power of attorney on the following accounts: CS 12345 in the name of Susie Smith; CS 34567 in the name of Jane Jones; and CS 67891 in the name of Joan Brown and John Doe. At the time he opened the accounts, Mr. Doe stated that he owned an antique shop in Any City. When asked about the reason for the joint accounts, Mr. Doe stated that he was trying to assist various friends and relatives with their asset management. Mr. Doe further advised a representative of our investment firm that Susie Smith was his common-law wife, Joan Brown was his cousin, and Jane Jones was his friend.

In addition to some securities trading, from February 2000 through November 2002, accounts CS 12345, CS 34567 and CS 67891 had total deposits of $923,709 and total withdrawals of $723,445. The accounts were funded in large part by personal checks issued on an account at XYZ Bank in the name of S. Smith, account number 9876543. The majority of the withdrawals from the three accounts consisted of checks made payable to 'cash' and endorsed by Mr. Doe and/or the other account holders.

On multiple occasions, Mr. Doe went to the Any City Branch office with checks from Ms. Smith's XYZ Bank account, in which the payee and amount of the checks were left blank. Mr. Doe then instructed his financial advisor as to the amount and payee of the checks. The financial advisor filled out those portions of the checks and deposited the checks on behalf of Mr. Doe into the appropriate brokerage account. When recently asked about the checking activity in the three accounts by a representative of our brokerage firm, Mr. Doe stated that the funds in the three accounts belonged to him and the withdrawals were made to cover his living expenses. Mr. Doe did not explain why he did not withdraw the cash directly from the XYZ Bank account.

A series of four checks were issued from account number CS 12345 on July 20, 2002, July 22, 2002, July 23, 2002 and July 25, 2002 in the amount of $8,000 each and were made payable to 'Michael Mouse, ESQ.' When asked about the checks by a representative of our brokerage firm, Mr. Doe stated that he owed money to Mr. Mouse but did not offer an explanation as to the reason the checks were issued several days apart.

In November 2002, Mr. Doe deposited into brokerage account CS 67891 four checks each in the amount of $5,000. The checks were dated November 6, 2002, November 7, 2002, November 8, 2002 and November 12, 2002, and were all drawn on an account at ABC Bank in the name of Daffine Duck. When asked about the checks by a brokerage firm representative, Mr. Doe stated that Ms. Duck is a fellow antique store owner who recently purchased a home. Mr. Doe added that he was advised that ABC Bank would not clear checks quickly if the total amount of checks for one day exceeded $5,000. The financial advisor filled out the payee and amount of the checks.

Our brokerage firm has restricted the accounts from any further activity and is the process of closing them. The financial advisor, Elmer Fudd, was terminated from the firm on November 29, 2002.

This SAR is filed due to the manner in which Mr. Doe handled transactions through the three brokerage accounts, the volume of funds in and out, especially the checks in July 2002 and the deposits in November 2002, in amounts that indicate possible structuring. All documentation related to this matter is retained in our firm's compliance office in Any City.

Comments:

This narrative answers the 5 "W's" (who?, what?, when?, where?, why?) of information by providing the names of individuals involved in the suspicious activity, the types of transactions and instruments involved, the time period and some specific dates of the activity, why the broker-dealer reported the customer, and the manner in which the activity was conducted. The planned action by the firm for the involved customers and accounts is stated. The narrative identifies where supporting documentation is maintained.

Insufficient or incomplete SAR-SF Narrative

Example # 1

> Account was opened in 2002. Assets were transferred in by wire. 50 checks for $250 were deposited, securities were liquidated and money was paid out in May 2003.

Comments:

This narrative provides no information to support the reason the broker-dealer submitted the SAR. Although some general transaction information is included, it fails to provide dates or amounts of the incoming credits to the account, i.e., the dates, amounts, originator, and source of the wire transfers, the issuer or issuers of the 50 checks, and the beneficiary of the funds closing the account in May. Also, no information is given concerning the owner of the account.

Examples of SARs Filed By Casinos and Card Clubs (SAR-Cs)

Sufficient and Complete SAR-C Narratives

Example #1

A SAR-C dated 11/03/2002 was previously filed on John Doe because of excessive wire transfers and minimal gambling activities. This supplemental report details recent suspect activities in which John Doe has engaged at Bob's Casino with other associates, Jack Doe and Jim Doe, which may indicate possible money laundering. The SAR-C is being filed based on numerous suspicious factors: 1. John Doe's excessive wire transfer activity; 2. John Doe's association with other players who are identified by the casino as having excessive incoming wires used to purchase chips; 3. Pass off of chips by Jack and Jim Doe to John Doe that are cashed out and deposited back into John Doe's account; and 4. Surveillance of Doe and associates, which indicate minimal play by all parties.

Specifically, the following wire transfers and patterns appeared suspicious. Between 10/12/2002 through 1/06/2003, John Doe has transacted wire transfers totaling $73,850 to Jane Doe, ABC Bank, account #12345678. The source of these funds was cashed-in chips. During the same time period, Jack Doe received four incoming wire transactions totaling $30,000 from Albert Doe, Bank of Good Fortune, New York, account #76543210. Jim Doe also received $40,000 from Albert Doe, Bank of Good Fortune, New York, account #765463210. Cash was taken from Jack and Jim Does' accounts for the purchase of chips. On five occasions as follows all three subjects were observed by Bob's Casino security playing black jack together at the casino: 10/12/2002, 10/20/2002, 11/02/2002, 11/03/2002, 12/17/2002 and 1/06/2003. Prior to each visit, Jack and Jim Doe receive wire transfers from Arnold Doe, which were used to purchase chips in increments of $6,000 to $8,000. John Doe purchased chips using a smaller balance maintained on his account, and was usually between $3,000 to $4,000. The black jack pit supervisor indicated each of the players did not extensively play but each took losses when they played between $300 to $500 each time they visited. The black jack supervisor has observed John Doe receiving chips from Jack and Jim Doe during some of their visits. The casino's surveillance of the subjects also confirmed observing the same type of activity between the patrons. John Doe normally deposited $14,000 to $17,000 in chips that he identified as winnings to pit clerks. Funds were usually wire transferred to Jane Doe on the day after John Doe visited the casino.

This matter has been referred to the State Gaming Commission and State Police. The investigation is ongoing.

Comments:

The narrative provides a detailed description of the suspicious activity and acknowledgement that a previous SAR-C was filed on the suspects. The conclusion of the narrative provides a clear disposition of the case in describing what the casino has done and is continuing to do in tracking the suspicious activities of the suspects.

Example #2

On June 27, 2003, Jane Smith came up to the third main cage and cashed out $5,000 in chips. She proceeded to hold purple chips (looked to be about $5,200) stating that she was going to keep those chips until later. While waiting in line, Ms. Smith was talking to another patron about the currency transaction reporting process and basically telling him how to avoid a CTR. She was explaining how the cage, table games, and slots compare their amounts and fill out a CTR when someone gets over $10,000. Ms. Smith told the other patron that's why she pulls some of her chips back so she will not have to pay taxes. She and the other gentleman then walked out together.

Ms. Smith has visited our casino over the last month, usually once a week. Her winnings were minimal until last week when on June 20, 2003 she cashed out $5,000 in chips one day. She returned the following day and cashed out an additional $5,000 in chips. We have maintained a copy of Ms. Smith's winnings over the last month and also a copy of her driver's license.

Today, Ms. Smith was informed that she was barred from our casino after she was overheard instructing another patron on how to avoid a CTR.

Comments:

The casino provides specific information in the narrative related to the actions by its patron, including dates and amounts of her transactions. It also includes her comments to other persons, which indicate her knowledge of the BSA CTR requirements and supports evidence of her own structuring efforts to evade these requirements.

Insufficient or incomplete SAR-C Narrative

Example #1

It appears that John Doe may have circumvented currency reporting procedures.

Comments:

The casino fails to provide any information to support this statement.

Made in the USA
Middletown, DE
22 October 2022

13306868R00020